MEETING GOD BEFORE

MORNING MOMENTS

THE DAY MEETS YOU

MEETING GOD BEFORE

MORNING MOMENTS

THE DAY MEETS YOU

ERICA TRIPLETT

Morning Moments by Erica Triplett.

ISBN: 979-8-9901758-9-1

Published in the United States by Yosi Publishing, LLC. For more inquiries or permissions, please contact the publisher at www.yosipublishing.com

Cover Design by Kai Holmes-Cooks of Kai & Co.

To my children, your patience and understanding have carried me through the years and have given me faith to be the best version of me.

Contents

Introduction XIII

1. Affirmed by the Creator 3
2. Created to Create 7
3. What Are You Wearing? 11
4. Grace to Stand 16
5. The Power of Confidence 20
6. Bruised but Useful 24
7. The Testing Phase 30
8. Don't Fear the Climb 34
9. The Strength to Wait 39
10. Called to Endure 44
11. When It Shakes: Earthquakes & Aftershocks 48
12. Through Waters & Fire 52
13. Let Go of Offense 58
14. Deep Cleaning 62
15. Root Canal Faith 66

16. Dealing Instead of Avoiding 70
17. Don't Pick It Up Unless It's a Promise 75
18. Guard the Gates 79
19. Be Mindful of the Time 84
20. What Ya' Thinking About? 88
21. Who Are You Listening To? 93
22. Stay in Your Lane 97
23. The Right Accessory 102
24. Roadmaps & Detours 106
SECTION FIVE 110
25. Favor & Understanding 111
26. Embrace the New 115
27. Be Like the Ducks 119
28. A Strong Tower 123
29. Don't Miss Your Appointed Time 127
30. Fear NOT 132
31. Unpacking Life's Suitcase 136
32. Obedience Wins Every Time 140
33. The Light at the End 144
34. Steer by the Seaman's Eye 148
35. Morning Mercies 152

Acknowledgements 158

About the Author 160

Introduction

This is the day the Lord has made. We will rejoice and be glad in it.— Psalm 118:24 NLT

I want to tell you something before we begin. God is not hiding from you.

He is not tucked away in the pages of theology books or reserved for Sunday mornings or extraordinary mountaintop experiences. He is right here—in the steam rising from your coffee cup, in the sunrise burning gold over the horizon, in the silence of a commute, in the unexpected kindness of a stranger. He is speaking in the small, sacred moments of your everyday life. The question is not whether He is present. The question is whether we have learned to look.

That is what this book is about.

I spent twenty years serving in the United States Navy, and one of the greatest gifts that season of life gave me was solitude at sea. In those quiet moments—standing on the deck watching the sun climb out of the water or sink back into it—I found God. Not in the grand or the dramatic, but in the breathtaking ordinary. Those were not special moments because anything spectacular had happened. They were special because I stopped long enough to notice. And in noticing, I began to hear. And in hearing, I began to see Him everywhere.

When I began sharing those moments—first in conversations, then on social media—something remarkable happened. People recognized themselves in them. They would say, "I've had that moment. I just didn't know that was God." That realization became the heartbeat of this devotional. So many of us are living in the middle of God's handiwork and missing it entirely—not because He is absent, but because we have not yet learned how to see Him in the everyday.

This devotional was written for you.

Whether you are a longtime believer or someone still finding your way toward faith, these thirty days were designed to meet you exactly where you are. You do not need to have it all figured out. You do not need a perfect prayer life or a theological degree. You only need a willingness to slow down, open your eyes, and begin.

How to Use This Book

Each of the thirt-five days follows the same rhythm, because the goal is not just to read about God—it is to build a daily practice of encountering Him.

- **Scripture.** Every day begins with God's Word. Before anything else, the scripture grounds you in truth and sets the tone for all that follows.

- **The Morning Moment.** A short devotional drawn from the real, relatable moments of everyday life—the kind you may have already experienced but perhaps never connected to God. These are not sermons. They are invitations to look again.

- **Prayer.** A guided prayer to help you respond to what you've read and carry it into the rest of your day.

- **Your Moment.** A dedicated space for you to write your own reflection. Where did you see God today? What ordinary moment spoke to you? This is your space to practice noticing.

The Journey Ahead

These thirty-five days are organized into six sections, each one a building block designed to carry you deeper into your daily walk with God:

- **Section 1: Foundations of Faith:** We begin where all things begin—with the bedrock truths that hold us when everything else shifts. Before you can see God in the everyday, you must know who He is.

- **Section 2: Trials and Endurance:** Faith is not tested in comfort. This section walks you through the hard moments and teaches you to find God not just in spite of them, but within them.

- **Section 3: Heart Work:** The deepest encounters with God happen when we allow Him into the places we have kept closed. This section invites you into honesty, healing, and surrender.

- **Section 4: Wisdom:** God speaks. He guides. He directs our steps. This section trains your ear to hear His voice in the still, small moments you might otherwise rush past.

- **Section 5: Favor:** You are seen. You are known. You are loved beyond measure. This section is a reminder of who you are to God—and what He has already set in motion on your behalf.

- **Section 6: Daily Living with God:** This is where everything comes together. Not a dramatic transformation, but a quiet, powerful shift in how you move through every single day—with God.

A Word of Challenge

I want to challenge you to do something that may feel unfamiliar at first: begin to intentionally reflect on your daily moments with God. Not just during your morning reading, but throughout the day. On your commute. In the middle of a hard conversation.

While watching something beautiful. In the moment you feel completely undone.

Ask yourself: *Where is God in this? What is He showing me? What is He saying?* Then write it down. Return to it. Let it become the language through which you begin to speak to God about your life, and through which He begins to speak back.

My prayer for you is simple and threefold: that this book brings you closer to God, that it heals something in your heart, and that it causes you to see Him working in everything—every single thing—in your life.

You are loved. You are seen. And you are walking into the newness of God.

Now let's begin.

With love and expectation,
Erica Triplett

SECTION ONE

FOUNDATIONS OF FAITH

One

Affirmed by the Creator

And God said, "Let there be light"; and there was light. God saw that the light was good (pleasing, useful) and He affirmed and sustained it; and God separated the light [distinguishing it] from the darkness. — Genesis 1:3–4 AMP

Have you ever found yourself looking for validation in everything except the right place? You go to your best friend hoping they'll approve your plans. You seek your parents' approval for your career choice. Or maybe you call your colleagues just to get their input on your next "big thing."

We've all been there waiting on someone's approval before we move forward. But this passage reminds us that the ultimate affirmation doesn't come from people; it comes from the Creator.

It says, *"God saw."* That means He looked at what He made—He examined it—and the Word says it was *pleasing and useful.* Then He affirmed it.

Affirmation from the wrong source can lead us into dangerous waters. So why not seek affirmation from the One who created us?

There was a time in my career when I was trying to be promoted and allowed the voice of others to affirm me in my position. It led me to believe I was all that I needed to be to receive the next promotion. When the time came for the promotion, I didn't meet the mark, matter of fact they presented me with a paper that said "FAIL". The same ones who were telling me how "great" I was, then determined I was not so great, and that I was in fact a failure. I wrestled with that for about three months and one day I was reminded that, *"God saw." And what He saw not only good, but He was able to sustain that which he saw.*

Think about it—do you think Steve Jobs needed everyone's approval before believing in himself? No! He knew what he created because he spent time perfecting it. In the same way, God—our Creator—crafted us, examined us, and declared, *"It is good." Jobs never gave up on his creation, just as God never gives up on us!*

Because He affirmed you, that settles it. You are *good, pleasing,* and *useful* in His eyes. You don't need another stamp of approval when Heaven has already signed off.

Morning Moment

Take a few minutes to sit quietly and ask God to show you what He sees when He sees you. Write it down and allow it to be a continuous reminder of who you truly are to God!

Prayer

Father, thank you for being intentional when you created me. I know who I am and what I can do because you looked at me and saw, I was good, pleasing in Your eyes, and useful. Your affirmation is all that I need in this walk, and I trust your word before others. Thank you for seeing me. In Jesus Name, Amen.

Two

Created to Create

In the beginning God created the heavens and the earth. — Genesis 1:1 NLT

Isn't it something that the God of all creation knows what it's like to create with *nothing*? That alone should bring us hope. The same God who spoke the world into existence understands what it feels like to have no visible resources and yet still create what was needed to fulfill His purpose.

We often feel like we're the first or only ones trying to build or create with limited means. But this verse shows us something powerful—the gift of creation doesn't require resources; it requires a mind to create.

"Needing something" is often just a trick of doubt that convinces us we can't move until we have more. But here in Genesis 1, God shows us that *with nothing,* He formed *everything.* And then, He kept creating!

So, what does that mean for you? It means what you desire to do—it's already in you. Don't focus on what you lack. Focus on what you *do* have: the thought, the idea, the vision, and the faith to begin. You were designed with the Creator's DNA. So, create anyway.

God gives us all the opportunity to join him in his creativity, but you must invite Him into that creative space with you. Let Him breathe on your ideas, inspire your hands, and multiply your efforts. You don't have to create *alone*—you get to create *with Him.* When you partner with the Creator, even the smallest beginning carries divine potential.

Morning Moment

This morning, think about that one idea or dream that you've put on hold. Write it down. Ask the Holy Spirit to give you one step you can take to begin creating with what you already have.

____

____

____

____

____

____

____

____

____

____

____

Prayer

Father, thank You for reminding me that You are the God who creates from nothing. When I feel like I don't have enough, help me to remember that all I need is the mind You gave me and the faith to move forward. I trust that as I create, you will breathe life into what I begin. In Jesus Name, Amen.

Three

What Are You Wearing?

So, chosen by God for this new life of love, dress in the wardrobe God picked out for you: compassion, kindness, humility, quiet strength, discipline. Be even-tempered, content with second place, quick to forgive an offense. Forgive as quickly and completely as the Master forgave you. And regardless of what else you put on, wear love. It's your basic, all-purpose garment. Never be without it. — Colossians 3:12–14 MSG

One of the biggest highlights on television is watching the Red Carpet. You see stunning gowns, elegant tuxedos, and sparkling jewels — and one of the first questions asked is always, *"What are you wearing?"* or *"Who are you wearing tonight?"*

That question can make or break a designer's career. An emerging designer can become a household name overnight, while an established one can lose influence if their creation doesn't shine.

I'll admit — I've found myself admiring what these men and women wear without ever considering *who* they really are underneath it all. It's easy to be captivated by the outer garment and overlook the heart of the person wearing it.

But that's something many of us do in our daily lives too. We carefully choose how we present ourselves—what others will *see* — while neglecting what truly matters: the garments of the heart. What we clothe ourselves in both naturally and spiritually is very intentional. You don't put on shorts when it's forecasted to snow, you grab the long sleeves and hoodies. It's the same for our spirit. When you're dealing with sickness, you intentionally pray to Rapha, the healer. When you are anxious, you should make it your purpose to read the scriptures to remind you what God says about being anxious.

Yes, it's true—when you look good, you feel good. But imagine how much *better* we'd feel if we "dressed" in compassion, kindness, humility, and patience. Those are the garments that never go out of style.

And above all, love is the ultimate accessory—the all-purpose garment that ties everything together.

So today, and every day after, let's dress intentionally. Let's wear the wardrobe God picked out for us—garments that reflect His nature and never lose their beauty.

Morning Moment

Stand before your closet or mirror and pray: "Lord, clothe me today in compassion, humility, and love." Write which "garment" you most need to wear more intentionally today and why.

Prayer

Lord, You are the greatest Designer. You know exactly what we should wear each day. Thank You for reminding us that our inner garments far outweigh what others can see. Teach us to be clothed in humility, compassion, strength, and most of all—love. May we never step out without wearing what You've chosen for us. In Jesus Name, Amen.

Four

Grace to Stand

And he gives grace generously. As the Scriptures say, "God opposes the proud but gives grace to the humble." So humble yourselves before God. Resist the devil, and he will flee from you. — James 4:6–7 NLT

Though the Lord is great, he cares for the humble, but he keeps his distance from the proud. — Psalm 138:6 NLT

The reality is — that isn't always the case. Grace isn't a license to do what we want; it's the power to live differently.

Grace is given to help us avoid the things that lead us into sin—disobedience, pride, or a haughty spirit—all which God dislikes. Psalm 138 reminds us that the Lord draws close to the lowly but keeps His distance from the proud.

Grace, then, becomes more than a concept. It is a divine strength, a gift given through the Holy Spirit that enables our lives to reflect both our faith *and* our salvation.

There have been so many times that grace has forced me to think differently and even live differently. It was grace that kept me when pride caused me to think I was doing the best that I could as a leader. I worked with and for many people who often didn't have the skillset that I had, but were in a higher position than I. I didn't always appreciate how that played out because they relied on my ability to execute while they collected all the accolades. It was grace and grace alone that allowed me to continue working in that environment. Which ultimately afforded be greater opportunities down the road.

What would your life look like if you truly submitted to the Father and received His grace in full?

Maybe—just maybe—it would reflect a life marked by humility, obedience, and steadfastness. A life that stands firm against anything that dares to oppose God and His grace.

Morning Moment

Ask God to reveal one area where pride has kept you from receiving His full grace. Write what He shows you and pray for humility and strength to surrender it to Him.

___

___

Prayer

Father, thank You for the gift of grace that teaches me how to walk humbly before You. Help me to live a life that reflects true submission, one that resists pride and embraces Your will. Keep me close to Your presence, and let Your grace be the strength that sustains me daily. In Jesus Name, Amen.

Five

The Power of Confidence

I pray that God, the source of hope, will fill you completely with joy and peace because you trust in him. Then you will overflow with confident hope through the power of the Holy Spirit. — Romans 15:13 NLT

Confidence—it's the firm belief that one can rely on someone or something. It's having *trust* that doesn't easily waver.

But sometimes, we lack confidence. We struggle to move, to wait, or even to believe. It's not always that we don't have faith—it's that fear tries to take faith's place. Yet today, here I sit, writing devotionals for a book.

The idea to publish a devotional has been told to me for years, but there was this lace of certainty that I struggled with. Matter of fact, I realized I was putting more on my own ability, than standing in the very confidence that Paul is talking about in this passage. When you take on confidence in God, you begin to overcome your lack and you begin to do things like, pick up the pen and write with an assurance that you will one day publish. You take the steps to not only join the gm, but to get up and go. That's what confidence in action looks like.

I'm praying for those who believe and trust but still wrestle with uncertainty, that you will do just what I have decided to do and pick up the pen, or whatever it is that has been calling you. Pick it up and run in full confidence that God is your source!

Lord, Your Word reminds us that You have not given us a spirit of fear. So today, we cast down fear and doubt, and we speak confidence. We place our trust in You and lean not on our own understanding.

Our hope is in You, Lord. Fill us with peace, joy, and unwavering confidence through the power of Your Holy Spirit. You are the everlasting God—the One who never fails.

We have *confidence* in knowing that You are still working miracles, keeping promises, still holding us in the palm of Your hand. Build us up in our most holy faith, Father, so that our confidence not only rests in receiving Your goodness but also in boldly *sharing* it with others.

Morning Moment

Write a declaration that begins, "Today I will move with confidence because..." Finish the sentence with what you believe God has spoken over your life. Repeat it aloud three times.

____

____

____

____

____

____

____

____

____

____

____

____

____

____

____

____

____

Prayer

God, thank You for being our source of hope. Strengthen our confidence in You today and remind us that fear has no place where Your Spirit dwells. Fill our hearts with peace, joy, and holy boldness to trust You completely. You are our Father, our Prince of Peace, and the anchor of our souls. We love You, and we stand firm in the confidence that You will never fail us. In Jesus Name, Amen.

Six

Bruised but Useful

The Lord gave another message to Jeremiah. He said, "Go down to the potter's shop, and I will speak to you there." So I did as he told me and found the potter working at his wheel. But the jar he was making did not turn out as he had hoped, so the potter crushed it into a lump of clay again and started over. Then the Lord gave me this message: "O Israel, can I not do to you as this potter has done to his clay? As the clay is in the potter's hand, so are you in my hand. —Jeremiah 18:1–6 NLT

When the cans in the store are dented, they're usually taken off the shelf or sold at a discount—even though what's inside hasn't changed one bit. The content remains the same; only the outside is flawed.

The same thing happens with a bruised piece of fruit. The store may toss it aside or hide it beneath the others, so no one sees it. But inside, it's still sweet.

Many of us know what it feels like to be "dented" or "bruised." Life hits hard.

I am reminded of how it felt after having a baby out of wedlock. I was very bruised and matter of fact, I had feelings of being less than because I had made myself feel as if I had sold myself cheap. I would play myself short and I would hide behind my bruises. I thought people were counting me out, until one day many years later, people begin to send other young ladies to me, to talk to them about being a mother who could raise a child on their own and still be successful. See, although I felt that I had messed up so much that I couldn't be used by God, he was taking my fragments, placing them back on the wheel and making me into the vessel that He needed me to be. Even in my brokenness and mess, God still found value in me.

Here lies the reality, people walk away. Mistakes leave marks. But the good news is this—God still sees what's *inside* of you. He knows that your value hasn't changed.

Just like the potter with the clay, God can reshape, restore, and use you again. The outside might look a little different, but what He placed inside of you from the beginning is still there—still usable, still filled with purpose.

I'm grateful to serve a God who sees beyond the dents, the bruises, and the broken places. He doesn't discard what others would throw away. Instead, He takes what's been marred and molds it into something even more beautiful than before.

Morning Moment

Close your eyes and picture yourself on the Potter's wheel. What part of your life feels misshapen or bruised right now? Write a short prayer surrendering that area to God's hands for remolding.

Prayer

Father, thank You for seeing value in me even when I feel dented, bruised, or overlooked. Remind me that what You placed inside of me still has purpose. Mold me, shape me, and use me for Your glory. Thank You for never throwing me away, but instead restoring me into something that brings You honor. In Jesus Name, Amen.

SECTION TWO

TRIALS & ENDURANCE

Seven

The Testing Phase

Beloved, do not be surprised at the fiery ordeal which is taking place to test you [that is, to test the quality of your faith], as though something strange or unusual were happening to you.— 1 Peter 4:12 AMP

Peter reminds us that testing is woven into the journey of sanctification; it is one of God's tools for spiritual growth.

Did you know that whenever you set a plan or make a declaration, it must be tested?

Think about it—have you ever decided to make a lifestyle change, like eating healthier, losing weight, or even setting a consistent bedtime? Before you said it out loud, you probably didn't realize how much you struggled in that area. But the moment you made the declaration—wrote it on your vision board or told someone your goal—here came the tests!

Suddenly, your job hosts bake sales every week, or your evenings fill up with errands that push your bedtime later and later. It's as if everything that could challenge your goal shows up all at once.

I call this the *testing phase* of your declaration. Just like a new product goes through a "beta phase" before being released, our faith goes through its own development process. During that time, the product is tested, refined, and adjusted—all to ensure it functions as intended.

God doesn't test us to break us, but because He is a wise and loving Father who knows exactly what He has placed within us. He is the potter, and we are the clay.

The same is true for us. Before God "releases" us to the next stage of purpose, He tests what's inside us. Just as Abraham had to trust God on the mountain with Isaac, his faith was proven through obedience under pressure. Our endurance, obedience, and consistency all go through refining fire and when God releases you, He positions you for influence, fruitfulness, and impact that aligns us with His purpose for our lives.

So, when the trials come, don't think it's strange. These tests are not meant to destroy you but to develop you. God is simply proving what He already placed within you—preparing you for release.

Morning Moment

Take one minute to identify a declaration you've recently made—big or small. Ask the Lord, "What are You refining in me through the tests surrounding this declaration?" Write down one area where He is strengthening your endurance today.

Prayer

Father, thank You for the tests that shape and strengthen me. Help me to see that my trials are not punishments but preparations. Give me the endurance to stand through the fiery moments and the faith to know You are refining me for greater purpose. Help me to focus on what You are doing in me, not just what's happening to me. In Jesus Name, Amen.

Eight

Don't Fear the Climb

I look up to the mountains—does my help come from there? My help comes from the Lord, who made heaven and earth! — Psalm 121:1–2 NLT

You don't go up and come back down the same way!

When you're climbing a mountain, the purpose of your journey can shift as you ascend. You may begin with one goal in mind—just reaching the top—but as you climb, things change. The air feels different. Your body adjusts. The atmosphere shifts.

And once you reach the top, your *view* changes too. What once looked big from below now seems small. What once felt overwhelming now appears insignificant. Higher ground gives you a new perspective—and perspective is what changes everything.

We can see this with Elijah on Mount Horeb, where God's whisper came after the climb, not before. Again, some clarity can only come at higher altitudes.

If you never ascend, you'll never see things from the place God intended. You'll miss the insight, wisdom, and clarity that only come from elevation.

Don't fear the climb because of how things may shift along the way. Embrace it! The ascent is God's intention for each of us. He desires that we see life from His view, and that only happens when we go higher. When God calls us higher, He is inviting us into deeper revelation, strengthened faith, and a clearer sense of His purpose.

If you've ever watched a mountain climber, you know the journey begins in the valley—often before sunrise. The climber carries a backpack filled with essentials for the trip. They may start with a group, but not everyone finishes the climb. Some grow weary or stop when the path gets steep. The valley is where we start, but the summit is where we see. In the valley we walk by faith; at the summit we see with understanding, and we hear with greater clarity.

Just like in mountain climbing, your spiritual climb may begin with many, but not everyone is called to climb at the same pace. Some people are only meant to journey part of the way, and guess what? THAT IS OKAY! Their stopping isn't rejection, and your continuance is not separation or a departure; it simply means God is leading and guiding each of you on your own paths.

You must pack your own bag—with faith, hope, and determination—and keep moving toward the summit. Because when you finally reach that place God is calling you to, you'll realize: your climb was never wasted.

Your climb may not be my climb, but if we're *climbing*, that's all that matters to God!

Morning Moment

Before your day begins, whisper this prayer: "Lord, lift my eyes higher." Picture yourself taking one step upward with Him. Write down one perspective shift you need today.

____

____

Prayer

Father, thank You for calling me to higher ground. Even when the climb feels steep, remind me that You are my help and my strength. Give me endurance for the journey and perspective for the process. Help me to see things the way You see them, and to never fear the changes that come with elevation. Thank You for being my help every step of the way. In Jesus Name, Amen.

Nine

The Strength to Wait

But those who trust in the Lord will find new strength. They will soar high on wings like eagles. They will run and not grow weary. They will walk and not faint. — Isaiah 40:31 NLT

Yet I am confident I will see the Lord's goodness while I am here in the land of the living. Wait patiently for the Lord. Be brave and courageous. Yes, wait patiently for the Lord. — Psalm 27:13–14 NLT

You've been in it long enough. It may not look like you're coming out, but today I'm praying for those who feel like throwing in the towel—yet every time you try, something within you won't let go.

God is whispering, "Just wait."

Waiting is the training ground where God shapes our endurance and deepens our total reliance on Him.

The promise is still in sight, even if your eyes can't yet see it. Your spirit senses what your vision can't capture—He's still working, and His light is still guiding. Soon, you'll not only see the path, but you'll walk boldly into the promise.

Remember: He is your light and salvation, your strength and shield. So do not fear—wait on Him, trust in Him, and know that He is faithful.

Israel knew what it meant to wait. They had a determination to make it to the promise land. It was a multiple generational wait that seemed delayed, but it was never denied. The children of Israel crossed over into their promised land, so shall your children cross over into theirs. When they do, they'll remember your steadfast faith and unwavering prayers.

When we wait, that does not mean we just sit and twiddle our thumbs. In fact, it is quite opposite of that. Waiting is alive and active. It causes us to learn to trust and even obey to simply, "just wait".

Let your confidence rise again today: you will see the goodness of the Lord in the land of the living.

Morning Moment

Sit still for sixty seconds. Breathe deeply and repeat: "God, I trust Your timing." Write one promise you are waiting to see come alive in your life.

Prayer

Father, thank You for reminding us that waiting is not wasted. When we grow weary, renew our strength. When we can't see the end, open our spiritual eyes to sense Your nearness. Help us to remain steadfast in faith, confident that Your promises will come to pass. Surround our children with Your angels and let them inherit the victories we've prayed for. We believe that we will see Your goodness—today and every day. In Jesus Name, Amen.

Ten

Called to Endure

Take with me your share of hardship [passing through the difficulties which you are called to endure], like a good soldier of Christ Jesus. — 2 Timothy 2:3 AMP

The best call to answer is the *call to endure!*

We love to talk about the calls that sound good — the ones that bring recognition or applause. The call to lead the conference. The call to spearhead the next big project. The call that makes us look accomplished and capable.

But what about the *hard* call? The one that doesn't come with accolades or public celebration. The one that makes you say, "Lord, You could've asked somebody else to do this!"

Paul's words to Timothy remind us that endurance isn't glamorous—it's gritty. It's the call to stay steady through hardship and difficulty. Endurance doesn't showcase your best moments; it exposes your breaking points. It doesn't highlight your strengths; it reveals the areas that still need refining.

Paul is a perfect example of being called to endure. He endured shipwrecks, prison, beatings, and betrayals. Many of us want to give up after one situation, but here we see, what true calling to endure looks like in the life of Paul.

But here's the blessing—endurance *pulls out* of you the very things that could cause you to fail. It forces out impatience, pride, fear, and doubt so that what remains is proven, pure, and strong. Endurance teaches us wisdom, grows us up and gives us strength that learns to stand when we would normally want to fall. Endurance shows us how to bear the fruit of the spirit.

When you answer the call to endure, you're saying yes to the process that leads to power. You're agreeing to let God shape you into someone who can stand, even when everything around you feels like it's falling apart. God never downplays what it cost to endure instead He promises to carry us through it.

So today if endurance is the call—answer it. It may not sound appealing, but it's the call that prepares you for every other one.

Morning Moment

Sit and think about what area(s) in your life that God is strengthening through endurance right now?

____

____

____

____

Prayer

Father, thank You for the strength to endure. When I'm called into hard seasons, help me to remember that You're developing me, not destroying me. Pull out anything in me that hinders my growth and build within me the resilience to stand firm. I trust that every hardship has purpose and that You're making me stronger for the journey ahead. In Jesus Name, Amen.

Eleven

When It Shakes: Earthquakes & Aftershocks

This means that all of creation will be shaken and removed, so that only unshakable things will remain. Since we are receiving a Kingdom that is unshakable, let us be thankful and please God by worshiping him with holy fear and awe. — Hebrews 12:27–28 NLT

Earthquakes happen when tectonic plates shift beneath the surface. That shifting causes a shaking that can be felt for miles. Whether it's small or large, the movement changes something—and its effects can last for days, months, or even years.

Life works much the same way. Many of us are experiencing a *shifting* and a *shaking* right now—unexpected changes, uncomfortable transitions, things moving that once felt stable. And much like an earthquake, it can catch us off guard.

But here's the truth: the shaking isn't random—it's *necessary.*

God sometimes allows the ground beneath us to move so that what is *unshakable* can remain. The shifting forces us to release what's temporary, unstable, or out of alignment with His will. It also makes room for what He's been preparing to build in its place. The shaking reveals the difference between what is Kingdom and what is everlasting.

Things may be moving; things may even be falling—but don't lose heart. The shaking won't last forever. You may feel a few aftershocks as the effects ripple out, but even that is part of the settling. In moments like these, steadiness comes through prayer, anchoring yourself in scripture, and making a choice to worship even when the ground seems to tremble.

Once the shaking quiets, you will find a new calmness because peace will always show up. The shaking and shifting were never meant to destroy you; they were designed to *position* you. What's being removed wasn't meant to stay, and what remains will be stronger than before.

Psalm 46 reminds us that even if the earth gives way, God is still our refuge and strength, our steady place in every shaking.

Morning Moment

Close your eyes and imagine placing every shaking situation into God's hands. Ask Him, "What are You stabilizing in me?" Write one truth that remains unshakable.

____

____

____

____

____

____

____

____

____

____

____

____

____

____

____

____

Prayer

Father, thank You for being steady even when everything around me feels unstable. Help me to trust You in seasons of shaking. Let every shift in my life align me closer to Your will. Remove what's temporary so that what's unshakable in You may remain. I know this shaking is necessary—and I thank You for using it to strengthen my foundation. In Jesus Name, Amen.

Twelve

Through Waters & Fire

When you pass through the waters, I will be with you; and through the rivers, they shall not overwhelm you; when you walk through fire you shall not be burned, and the flame shall not consume you. — Isaiah 43:2 ESV

The Singer Chaka Kahn sang a song, and the lyrics were, "Through the fire, to the limit to the wall, for a chance to be with you, I'd gladly risk it all...right down to the wire, even through the fire" And though she was singing about a romantic relationship, this is how God sees each of us in our trials. It is a reflection of God's convent faithfulness.

We can all consider the hardest things that we may have gone through and who we experienced it with. Whether it is with people or with God, we will all go through trials. But who we go through them with, makes a grave difference in how we go through.

One of the hardest diagnoses in life is the one that starts with the C. Yes, CANCER. That word is gut wrenching and leaves us to immediately think of the possibility of dying and for some that is their fate. I am sure many of you have had those near and dear to you get that call and hear those words. The one thing that many attest to being able to make it through that experience, is that they had the love and support. For some that isn't always the case, and it often reflects in their healing process.

When we are going through trials, not only is a faith being tested, but so is our relationship with the one who walks us through. Suffering through trials with someone who wants you to make it, brings a sense of deeper love that only can be found in a tough situation.

Crossing rivers and making it out of fiery situations is never meant to be easy, it isn't designed for survival. It is made for destruction, but because God is with us, this biblical promise gives us hope. Hope that no matter what, if God is in it with us, then we will be alright.

Life isn't meant to be trial free. It isn't meant to be without experiences that bring us to our knees. It is meant to be lived with a hope and trust in the God who walks through the fire with us!

Morning Moment

Reflect on the smallest trial you have been in and then reflect on the biggest trial. Write down how God was with you in each of those moments.

Prayer

Father, thank you for always being with me. Whether it is in the fire or whether it is in the river. You are there. Lord, allow me to never forget that you are near, allow me to always remember that you are with me and no matter how the water gets or how hot the fire feels, I will endure and make it out because the flame shall not consume me. In Jesus Name, Amen.

SECTION THREE

HEART WORK

Thirteen

Let Go of Offense

Make allowance for each other's faults and forgive anyone who offends you. Remember, the Lord forgave you, so you must forgive others. — Colossians 3:13 NLT

The posture of offense is often mistaken for a posture of protection—a way to keep ourselves from being hurt again. But when it comes to matters of the heart, offense doesn't protect; it imprisons.

Have you ever experienced so much hurt and heartache that you simply stay on the offensive? It's like you walk into every room already bracing yourself, feeling like everyone is watching, judging, or misunderstanding you. Truth is—you've just picked up something that doesn't belong to you: the *spirit of offense.*

I said *picked it up* because that means you can also put it down.

The heart, when left unchecked, will deceive us into thinking that everyone is against us. We end up holding people hostage for offenses they never committed. We carry old wounds into new relationships, friendships, and even ministries.

But God's Word reminds us to *forgive anyone who offends you*. In other words—drop it!

Here is the thing, He isn't asking us to do so blindly. He asks us to do so just as he first forgave us. That kind of forgiveness should be emulated and is a well that we each can draw from. Jesus, there on the cross, demonstrates this when He cries out, father forgive them, for they do not know what they are doing, He in this state of crucifixion, torment, and even death, was able to let it go!

Let it go. Let it go!

Even Elsa from *Frozen* figured this out—if she didn't release what was freezing her heart, she couldn't walk fully in her gift. Likewise, if we don't let go of offense, fear, and resentment, we block what God wants to do in and through us. Offense doesn't just ruin wound your heart, its hiders your purpose and keeps you stagnant.

So today, take the first step toward your freedom. Drop it and let it go. This is how God begins His true work in your heart.

Morning Moment

Pause for a moment and ask: "Lord, who or what am I still carrying?" Write down one offense you choose to release today, and declare out loud, "I drop it and give it to God."

____

____

____

Prayer

Father, thank You for showing me that holding onto offense only hinders my growth. Today, I choose to release the pain, the people, and the situations that have wounded me. Help me to forgive quickly, to love freely, and to walk in peace. Teach my heart to let go so that You can freely work in and through me. I lay it all at Your feet—every offense, every hurt, every fear. In Jesus Name, Amen.

Fourteen

Deep Cleaning

Search me, O God, and know my heart; test me and know my anxious thoughts. Point out anything in me that offends you, and lead me along the path of everlasting life. — Psalm 139:23–24 NLT

Deep cleaning is one of my least favorite things to do.

It requires me to investigate places I'd rather skip over—the corners, under the furniture, the spaces I usually move around and pretend not to see. It's the kind of work that makes you get down on your knees and deal with what's been ignored. But the truth is—it *needs* to be done.

And the same is true in life. We all have areas in our hearts we'd rather skim over—the ones we hide behind excuses or box up and tuck away in the back of our minds. It feels easier to avoid them than to face what's there.

But just like a house that hasn't been cleaned deeply in a while, those neglected spaces in our hearts start to gather dust—old hurt, bitterness, pride, fear, and regret. These can be hidden faults that we pretend aren't there; unforgiveness, resentment etc.

When David prayed, *"Search me, O God,"* he was inviting the ultimate deep clean—asking God to reveal the hidden things and help him deal with them. Sometimes, that requires us to get down on our knees too—literally and spiritually—and let God wipe away the buildup. It is then, that the Holy Spirit can get to those hidden things and restore that which has been covered.

God's deep cleaning isn't condemning, its restoring! He removes the dirt, so that our joy and peace can return.

It may not be springtime, but a good cleaning can bring new life at *any* time. Today, ask God to help you do some heart cleaning. It might be uncomfortable at first, but afterward...you'll breathe easier.

David's prayer is an invitation that we should open to God consistently.

Morning Moment

Ask God to shine His light on one area of your heart you've overlooked. Write down whatever He brings up—just one thing—and invite Him to begin cleansing that space today.

___

___

___

___

Prayer

Father, search my heart and reveal what I've been avoiding. Help me not to skip over the areas that need Your touch. Cleanse me from hidden faults and renew the places I've neglected. I give You permission to do a deep clean in me — not just to make me look better, but to make me whole. In Jesus Name, Amen.

Fifteen

Root Canal Faith

He cuts off every branch of mine that doesn't produce fruit, and he prunes the branches that do bear fruit so they will produce even more. —John 15:2 NLT

Sometimes God is trying to pull you out of something, but the roots are so deep that He must dig through the dirt and get right to the source before He can bring you out.

We often tell ourselves, *"If God didn't want me in this, He would have pulled me out by now."* But that's not always how He works. Just because you're *in it* doesn't mean you're meant to *stay* in it.

If God were to pull you out too soon, a piece of the root might remain—and that same root could regrow once you're replanted in new soil. Sometimes He must dig deep, expose what's beneath the surface, and deal with what's been hidden before the true healing and growth can happen. As painful as this may be, it is never meant to harm us. Matter of fact, it is an act of love. Hebrews 12:6 reminds us that the Lord disciplines those He loves. In other words, while he is digging around, he is trying to be sure that we g row.

Hannah experienced this when God met her at the point of her need in her grief. He had to help her to deal with the deeper issue before He could open her womb. Once this was done, then the promise was released.

This is what I call *Root Canal Faith*—the kind of faith that endures when God must go beneath the surface to remove what's decayed, what's attached, and what no longer belongs.

It may hurt. It may feel like too much. But when God finishes, there will be no residue of the old you—only fresh soil, new growth, and fruit that lasts.

Ask yourself, what is God digging up in this season, so He cab replant you in something better?

Morning Moment

Take a quiet moment and ask the Lord, "What root are You revealing so You can heal me?" Write down the first word or phrase that comes to mind.

____

____

____

____

____

____

Prayer

Father, thank You for caring enough to dig deep. Even when the process is uncomfortable, help me to trust that You're removing what no longer serves my growth. Uproot anything that keeps me bound and replant me in good soil where I can thrive and bear lasting fruit. In Jesus Name, Amen.

Sixteen

Dealing Instead of Avoiding

Don't worry about anything; instead, pray about everything. Tell God what you need, and thank him for all he has done. Then you will experience God's peace, which exceeds anything we can understand. His peace will guard your hearts and minds as you live in Christ Jesus. — Philippians 4:6–7 NLT

Give all your worries and cares to God, for he cares about you. — 1 Peter 5:7 NLT

There are some assignments meant to be finished *in class* and others you take *home.* In life, we often mix the two — carrying home what was never meant to leave the classroom.

Some things God only meant for us to handle in the moment, but instead, we pack them up, take them with us, and let them linger far too long.

Recently, I realized I'd been home from a trip for over two weeks… and still hadn't unpacked my suitcase. (Don't judge me — judge ya mama, as the kids say!) I kept rolling it around the room instead of just dealing with it.

Then it hit me — that's how we handle life. We keep emotional "suitcases" packed with things we should've already unpacked. Avoidance feels easier, but it only delays peace. It builds us like clutter and crowds our thoughts, drains our energy, and steals every good thought.

Jonah was willing to avoid what he had been instructed to do, that he ran away. In his avoidance, he found himself in a greater dilemma with greater consequences not only for him, but for others. It was when he decided to deal with what was in front of him that there was peace in the storm.

The moment we obey, we receive peace. The kind of peace that cannot be described.

What is the one thing that you have been avoiding and keeping packed away? It might be time to start unpacking.

Today, I'm choosing to unpack — one thing at a time — and give it to God. Maybe for you it's tomorrow, but when you do, you'll feel lighter. There's freedom in *dealing instead of avoiding.*

Morning Moment

Write down one "suitcase item" you've been avoiding—fear, grief, disappointment, or worry. Whisper this prayer: "Lord, I hand this to You today."

Prayer

Father, help me to stop carrying what You never asked me to. Give me courage to unpack the things I've avoided and peace to leave them in Your hands. In Jesus Name, Amen.

Seventeen

Don't Pick It Up Unless It's a Promise

Let us hold tightly without wavering to the hope we affirm, for God can be trusted to keep his promise.
— Hebrews 10:23 NLT

I have realized how easily I pick things up that were never mean for me to carry. Worries, opinions, the stress of those around me. It is as if I like to carry additional weight that wasn't for me to carry.

This savior mentality that is often picked up seems to cause many of us to believe that we are to carry burdens when God only asked us to carry promises.

When you are working on yourself and becoming a better you, there is a gift of discernment that you must ask God to help you cultivate. Not everything is designed for you to carry and much of the weight that we often are trying to shoulder, isn't for us.

There are truths and promised that we are to pick up along the way that allow us to lean on God more than we lean on our own thoughts and our own ways of thinking,

Imagine having your hand full of the promises of God and imagine having your other hand full of the burdens. Do you think God would rather you hold on to his promises or to the burden? I believe it is the promises, because in his promises we have a Yes and Amen.

Morning Moment

Take a moment and think about what you are carrying today. Is it truly yours to carry? Below, write down one burden you have been holding onto—then write beside it one promise of God that speaks directly to it. Practice the exchange. Let His promise be the thing your hands hold tightly to today.

____

____

____

____

____

____

____

____

____

____

Prayer

Lord, today I come to You with open hands. I acknowledge that I have been carrying things You never asked me to hold — worries that are not mine, burdens that belong to You, weight that was never designed for my shoulders. Forgive me for the times I have trusted my own strength over Your promises. Right now, I make the exchange. I lay down every burden, every fear, every opinion and stress I have picked up along the way, and I choose to pick up Your promises instead. Teach me the gift of discernment — to know what is mine to carry and what is Yours to handle. Let Your Word be the anchor I hold when everything around me feels heavy. I trust that You are faithful, that Your promises are yes and amen, and that I never have to carry more than what You have graced me to hold. Thank You for being a God who keeps every promise He makes. In Jesus Name, Amen.

Eighteen

Guard the Gates

Guard your heart above all else, for it determines the course of your life. Avoid all perverse talk; stay away from corrupt speech. Look straight ahead and fix your eyes on what lies before you. — Proverbs 4:23–27 NLT

Your ears, your eyes, your mind, and your heart. These places are where information is received, processed, and stored and leads to the way our lives are shaped. Scripture teaches that whatever enters through these gates, eventually settles in the heart.

Your ears control what you hear—and even when you don't agree with what's being said, those words can still find their way into your mind. If left unchecked, they can shape your thoughts about yourself or others. And let's not mention how the wrong vices can distort our identity, influence our decisions, and pull us off the path God has set before us.

That's why it's so important to turn the volume down—to the right decibel—so you can hear what *really* matters. There's so much noise around us that doesn't belong in our spirit. When we let it in, it clouds our judgment, interrupts our thought patterns, and weakens our effectiveness in the very gifts God gave us—the ones someone else may be depending on for their breakthrough.

Sometimes guarding your gates means taking a step back from the crowd and loudness. Logging out of social media, refusing to let gossip get in your spirit, and ignoring the temptation to compare your life to others,

So today, take time to quiet the noise. Let your heart be still—His temple again.

As I sat in morning worship, I was reminded how overwhelming His love and grace truly are. God's presence fills every empty place, and His faithfulness never changes. Even when it feels like He's far away, He gently reminds me that He's been there all along.

Each day brings brand-new mercies—and the peace that comes when we turn down the world's volume to hear His voice clearly.

Morning Moment

Sit in silence for one minute. Ask God, "What noise do I need to turn down today so I can hear You clearly?" Write down the answer.

____

____

____

____

____

Prayer

Father, help me to tune my ear to Your voice and quiet everything that distracts me. Let my heart stay pure and open to Your guidance. Thank You for Your unfailing love and the peace that comes when I rest in You. In Jesus Name, Amen.

SECTION FOUR

WISDOM & PERSPECTIVE

Nineteen

Be Mindful of the Time

For everything there is a season, a time for every activity under heaven. — Ecclesiastes 3:1 NLT

This morning while getting ready, I realized it was almost eight o'clock and I hadn't heard my son moving. I called out to him, reminding him that we leave at 8:15. A few moments passed—still no sound. Finally, I said, *"Son, you have to get ready and be mindful of the time."*

That small exchange reminded me how often we miss *appointed moments* in life—not because we're incapable, but because we're not mindful. Being mindful doesn't mean to rush or to worry, rather it is spiritual awareness in noticing the moments God has placed in front of us.

God orders every season and sets the timing for every moment in our lives. Mindfulness is simply noticing what He has arranged.

Just as we need to be aware of the hour, we also need to be aware of our thought. This teaches us how to naturally shape our focus as well as our thinking.

Our minds are powerful. They can keep us bound by dwelling on what hasn't happened, or they can release us into purpose by focusing on what's true, lovely, and praiseworthy (Philippians 4:8). What we think about shapes how we move—and sometimes, delays are less about timing and more about thought patterns.

Be mindful of what fills your mind. Choose to focus on growth instead of regret, progress instead of perfection, and lessons instead of losses. Because with pure motives and right intentions, you never really lose—you *learn.*

Morning Moment

Ask the Lord, "What season am I in right now?" Write one word that describes where God has you, and onc way to honor that season today.

Prayer

Father, help me to be mindful of the time You've set for me. Teach me to guard my thoughts and focus on what is true, lovely, and worthy of praise. When I feel delayed or distracted, draw my attention back to You. Thank You for reminding me that every season has purpose—and so do I. In Jesus Name, Amen.

Twenty

What Ya' Thinking About?

And now, dear brothers and sisters, one final thing. Fix your thoughts on what is true, and honorable, and right, and pure, and lovely, and admirable. Think about things that are excellent and worthy of praise. — Philippians 4:8 NLT

Have you ever considered your thoughts—and the power they hold?

Think about how often you scroll through social media and notice how the algorithm seems to know exactly what to show you. That algorithm reflects your patterns of thought. It reveals what you're drawn to, what you dwell on, and where your focus tends to land.

Just like digital algorithms respond to what we engage with, Scripture teaches that our lives respond to what we meditate on. Joshua 1:8 reminds us that we keep God's word before us, it shapes our direction and prospers our way.

Are your thoughts centered on the next best recipe, the dream vacation, or something deeper—like peace, purpose, and joy? Whatever your thoughts are, they shape what y ou *see*—in both the natural and the spiritual.

James Allen, in his classic book *As a Man Thinketh*, describes the mind as a *garden* where our thoughts are seeds. It's a timeless principle, but it was biblical first. Paul builds that truth by instructing us to think about things that are pure, lovely, admirable, and worthy of praise.

Whatever we plant, we eventually harvest. New thoughts will lead to a cultivation of new outlooks.

Imagine if your mental garden was always blooming with life-giving thoughts—hope, faith, kindness, creativity, and love. What beauty would grow from that soil? What peace would fill your heart?

The power of a thought is that it multiplies. So, keep your thoughts rooted in goodness, just as God's thoughts toward you are pure, lovely, and full of excellence.

So, ask yourself today:

- *What are you growing in your mind?*
- *And is it driving your spiritual algorithm toward faith or fear?*

Morning Moment

Write one thought that has been dominating your mind. Then write a Philippians 4:8 thought that can replace it.

Prayer

Father, thank You for giving me the ability to think and to create through my thoughts. Help me to fix my mind on what is true, noble, pure, and lovely. Uproot every seed of negativity and doubt, and plant within me thoughts that honor You. Let my mind reflect Your peace and produce fruit that brings glory to Your name. In Jesus Name, Amen.

Twenty-One

Who Are You Listening To?

My sheep hear my voice, and I know them, and they follow me. —John 10:27 ESV

Have you ever been in the airport, and you were trying to listen to all of the conversations going on around you? I mean, you are listening to the mother lecturing her child about running all over the place, you are listening to the man on his phone with his boss about the project that didn't get completed on time. I mean you are so in tune with these side bar conversations, that you don't hear the agent announce that your flight has been moved to a different gate.

It is something about the attentiveness of our ear that causes us to have an ability to hear multiple things at once, but at the same time miss out on the key things we should be listening to.

A Shepard spends an extensive amount of time with his sheep in order to get them into a rhythm of knowing their voice. The value in this is that they won't be led astray by just any voice or voices.

What is the importance in this? It is a protective measure to shield from hurt, injury, or simply being ked astray.

Think about it, Abraham heard the voice of God and did what he heard, and this led him to becoming the father of nations. Noah heard the voice of God and it led to the redeeming power of mankind. Even Moses, hearing the voice of God led to the deliverance of the people out of Egypt.

This did not come because they just had a keen ear. This came because of relationship. Relationship built on prayer, intimate time in the presence of God.

What would it look like if we spent so much time with God that we heard him speak and obeyed the first time? We would look like the Abrahams, and Moses' of our own day,

Morning Moment

Ask the Lord: "whose voice have I been obeying?" Write the first impression the Holy Spirit brings.

____

____

____

____

____

____

____

____

Prayer

Father, you are the Good Shephard, and your voice is the only voice that I desire to follow. Teach me how to not allow the noise around me to distract me from hearing and doing what you say to do. Lord, when I fall and listen to the others, forgive me and try me again. In Jesus Name, Amen.

Twenty-Two

Stay in Your Lane

Therefore, since we are surrounded by such a huge crowd of witnesses to the life of faith, let us strip off every weight that slows us down, especially the sin that so easily trips us up. And let us run with endurance the race God has set before us. — Hebrews 12:1 NLT

I don't mean to say that I have already achieved these things or that I have already reached perfection. But I press on to possess that perfection for which Christ Jesus first possessed me. No, dear brothers and sisters, I have not achieved it,[a] but I focus on this one thing: Forgetting the past and looking forward to what lies ahead, **14** *I press on to reach the end of the race and receive the heavenly prize for which God, through Christ Jesus, is calling us.— Philippians 3:12–14 NLT*

"*You ran well, but what hindered you?"* — Bishop Ezekiel Williams

This question, posed to us during a midweek worship service, has continued to ring in my ear over the years. Hinderance can look like a lot of things—distractions, discouragement, comparison, or anything that shifts our focus from the lane God assigned us to.

When my son started running track, his coach wouldn't allow the team to collect medals after events. At first, I didn't understand why. I thought the medals were a sign of progress. But as the season went on, I noticed something—the athletes weren't talking about medals anymore. They were talking about *PR-ing*—setting a *personal record.*

Curious, I asked the coach why. He said, "If they focus on winning medals instead of improving, then what happens when they run a slower time? But if they focus on being better than before, they'll always win—even without a medal."

That revelation stuck with me.

The Word tells us to run our race so that we may obtain the prize. But the true prize isn't the applause or recognition—it's growth, endurance, and hearing "Well done" at the finish line. See God measures faithfulness, not speed. Your continuous obedience matters far more than how quickly you finish.

Sometimes we get distracted, looking at who's ahead, who's behind, or what others are achieving. But your race is *your race.* God isn't measuring you against anyone else—He's looking for improvement, faithfulness, and obedience in *your lane.*

Don't let comparison or competition become your hindrance. Run with focus, grace, and the filter of assignment. Every step you take, every test you overcome, every season you endure—it's all progress in God's eyes.

He's not after medals. He's after movement. Take a moment and ask yourself: What is hindering me in this season? What us pulling my attention away from my own lane?

Morning Moment

Ask yourself: "What is pulling me out of alignment today?" Write one step you will take to stay in your lane.

Prayer

Father, thank You for the race You've set before me. Help me to stay focused on my own lane and not be distracted by others. Teach me to find joy in progress, not comparison, and to run each race with endurance and grace. When I cross the finish line, I only want to hear You say, "Well done." In Jesus Name, Amen.

Twenty-Three

The Right Accessory

Yes, I am the vine; you are the branches. Those who remain in me, and I in them, will produce much fruit. For apart from me you can do nothing. —John 15:5 NLT

If you've ever used an Apple product, you've probably seen the message: *"This accessory is not supported by this device."*

Apple products are particular — intentionally designed to work best when connected to compatible accessories. If a charger or cable isn't Apple-certified, the device won't recognize it as a valid source of power. The reason? It might be damaged, off-brand, or incompatible.

The same is true with our spiritual connection. We were designed and created in God's image—which means not every source of "power" will fit us. We can't plug into everything and expect to stay charged.

Not every connection is filled with power; some are counterfeits disguised as strength sent to drain you of what power you do have.

Some connections may look right, sound right, or even feel right for a moment, but if they're not *God-approved*, they won't sustain us. There's a distinction between being connected and being *properly* connected. Fruit doesn't come from striving; it comes from abiding. When you remain in Him, the growth flows naturally. There isn't a force to produce, you just simply bear.

Stay plugged into the true Source—the Vine. Because when your power comes from Him, you'll never get the message, *"This accessory is not supported."*

Morning Moment

Write one sentence completing this phrase: "Lord, today I choose to stay connected to You by ________.

____

____

____

____

____

____

____

____

____

____

____

____

Prayer

Father, thank You for being my true Source. Help me to stay connected to You and disconnect from anything that drains or distracts me. Keep me rooted in Your presence so that everything I produce brings glory to You. In Jesus Name, Amen.

Twenty-Four
Roadmaps & Detours

For I know the plans I have for you," says the Lord. "They are plans for good and not for disaster, to give you a future and a hope. —Jeremiah 29:11 NLT

When roads were first established, someone had to *survey the land*—to study waterways, mountains, and natural obstacles—to determine the safest and most effective route toward the destination.

What if I told you that Someone is still surveying the path for your life?

I'm amazed at the roads that have been laid out for me, but even more amazed that my *destination* is so important to God that nothing can stop me from reaching my expected end.

Roadmaps can help others travel toward similar destinations, but that doesn't mean everyone will arrive at the same time or in the same condition. Progression isn't a cookie cutter way. There's bends and turns that leads us differently, but always brings us to our destination of hope and promise in God.

Just because you're on the same road as someone else doesn't mean your journey will look identical. You may face detours, slowdowns, or even a few accidents along the way—but the beauty is, you're still *moving. We tend to look at detours as a delay in our travel, and that's not always the case. They can lead you along a greater path with a broader chance to see the roads traveled from a different route.*

It's not about how fast you get there or how smooth the road feels—it's about *arriving.*

Keep driving. Keep pushing. Keep moving forward on the road God has surveyed for you. The destination is already set.

Morning Moment

Ask God: "What detour in my life have You been using for my good?" Write down the answer and thank Him for guiding your path.

____

____

____

____

____

____

____

____

____

____

____

____

Prayer

Father, thank You for being the Master Surveyor of my path. Even when the road gets rough, remind me that You've already planned my destination. Help me stay the course with patience and trust, knowing that every turn, delay, and detour is leading me exactly where You've designed me to be. In Jesus Name, Amen.

SECTION FIVE

FAVOR & NEWNESS

Twenty-Five

Favor & Understanding

And so find favor and high esteem in the sight of God and man. Trust in the Lord with all your heart, And lean not on your own understanding; In all your ways acknowledge Him, And He shall direct your paths. — Proverbs 3:4–6 NKJV

"Favor is a lifestyle of ever-increasing, ever-expanding preference that upgrades our relationship with the Godhead and our status in the Kingdom. The development of favor goes together with learning the art of walking out and working in the truth of who Christ is for us and who we have permission to become in Him. Favor is best received as part of a joyful process that enables us to contend against our own negativity and overcome every circumstance of life because we have found favor in the eyes of God." — Graham Cook

Favor flows from God's grace, not our striving. There isn't anything we can do to earn it because it is rooted in relationship with Christ.

We often talk about *favor* as the highlight—the blessing, the open door, the opportunity. But we tend to skip over the equally important part of the verse: *"and good understanding."*

Understanding equals *wisdom*, and wisdom is essential to *sustain* favor. Without it, we may mismanage what we've been graced to receive.

Favor without wisdom is like rain with no soil—it falls, but it doesn't produce. Wisdom gives favor direction, depth, and purpose.

Solomon was a man who received favor, but his asking was for wisdom! Without wisdom to manage favor, you would be lost with what to do.

So, ask yourself today: Now that you've found favor — what will you do with it? Use it well. Steward it with humility.

Morning Moment

Take a mental picture of the favor you've received in the last year, and ask yourself, how you have stewarded it.

____

____

____

Prayer

Father, thank You for Your favor. Help me to walk in wisdom so that I can manage the blessings You entrust to me. Teach me to use favor not for recognition, but for impact—to bring glory to Your name and advancement to Your Kingdom. In Jesus Name, Amen.

Twenty-Six

Embrace the New

But forget all that—it is nothing compared to what I am going to do. For I am about to do something new. See, I have already begun! Do you not see it? — Isaiah 43:18–19 NLT

This means that anyone who belongs to Christ has become a new person. The old life is gone; a new life has begun! — 2 Corinthians 5:17 NLT

"I wanna be new, I wanna be just like You, Jesus, bring new wine out of me."— *Brooke Ligertwood*

If you haven't listened to *The Encounter* album by Todd Galberth, you're missing out on a worship experience filled with powerful moments — but one song that's been on repeat for me for months is *"New Wine."*

Many of us are familiar with the imagery—the crushing, the pressing of grapes to produce wine, and the idea that new wine must be poured into new wineskins. But have we really stopped to consider what it means when we ask, *"God, bring new wine out of me"*?

When we make that declaration, we're inviting God into the process—not just the *outcome.* We're saying, "Lord, if You must crush what's comfortable, press what's hidden, and stretch what's old to bring out something new in me...do it."

The newness we long for doesn't come without surrender. It's in the pressing that purpose is purified, and in the crushing that character is created. New wine requires a *new vessel*—one that's been renewed, reshaped, and ready to contain the fullness of what God is pouring out.

So today, don't just sing the words. Live them. Let God make you new—not just refined, but *reborn.*

Morning Moment

Where have you felt God crushing you? Reflect on that and write down what he may be trying to bring out from that crushing.

____

____

____

____

____

____

____

Prayer

Father, thank You for the new thing You're doing in my life. Even when it requires pressing or crushing, help me to trust that You're producing something greater within me. Make me new, reshape my heart, and pour out Your Spirit in me like new wine. In Jesus Name, Amen.

Twenty-Seven

Be Like the Ducks

Look, I have given you authority over all the power of the enemy. Nothing will harm you. — Luke 10:19 NLT

We were created so that God could fellowship with us—to sit in His goodness, behold His beauty, and simply *be* with Him. One of the principles of creation is this: when God made it, He looked at it and said, *"It is good."*

So why wouldn't we take moments in our day to slow down, look around, and enjoy what's good— to commune with the One who made it all?

This morning, I saw something that made me think. The level of authority that ducks walk in is impeccable!

They'll waddle straight into moving traffic, confident that not one car will interfere with where they're headed. Traffic comes to a complete stop, drivers swerve, and people risk missing green lights—all to avoid hitting them. (This is the *second* day I've seen this!)

And the best part? They don't walk alone—they bring others with them. That's authority.

Those ducks know exactly who they are and where they're going, and nothing—not even oncoming traffic—can stop them.

So today, *be like the ducks.* Walk boldly in the authority God has given you. Keep moving forward, no matter what's coming at you. And while you're at it, take someone with you.

Morning Moment

Is God showing you a place that you are afraid to walk boldly? Spend some time asking him how you can get to that place of authority and boldness.

____

____

____

____

____

____

____

Prayer

Father, thank You for giving me authority through Christ. Help me to walk boldly and confidently in Your power. Teach me to move forward without fear, to recognize my worth, and to encourage others along the way. Thank You that no obstacle can stop what You've ordained. In Jesus Name, Amen.

Twenty-Eight

A Strong Tower

The name of the Lord is a strong tower; the righteous man runs into it and is safe. — Proverbs 18:10 ESV

There are moments in life when everything around you feels uncertain. When the ground beneath you shifts and the noise of the world grows loud. In those moments, you do not need a plan—you need a name.

Jehovah. The self-existing One. The God who was, and is, and is to come. His name alone is a fortress. Not a feeling, not a circumstance, not the opinion of those around you—His name. And the beautiful thing about a strong tower is that you do not have to build it. You simply have to run to it.

When fear comes, run to His name. When doubt creeps in, run to His name. When the weight of life feels too heavy to carry, you have a place to go—and it will never fall.

Morning Moment

What are you running to today instead of running to God? Write down the one thing pulling your attention away from Him—then write His name beside it as your answer.

Prayer

Lord, remind me today that Your name is enough. When I am afraid, when I am overwhelmed, when I don't know what to do—let my first instinct be to run to You. You are my strong tower and I am safe in You. In Jesus' Name, Amen.

Twenty-Nine

Don't Miss Your Appointed Time

For still the vision awaits its appointed time; it hastens to the end—it will not lie. If it seems slow, wait for it; it will surely come; it will not delay. — Habakkuk 2:3 ESV

Imagine investing years on a job being someone else's number 2, when you know in fact, you could be the lead. Or what about being in a relationship that you believe has not produced anything more than heartache and headache. Over time, it's easy to believe those years were wasted.

These are valid thoughts, but anything we surrender to God can be beneficial to our process.

What we believe is delay is typically development. What looked like being passed over, really was God ordering your steps and divine appointment.

What we do in these seasons matters. When we allow God to truly perfect us and prepare us for our appointed times, we can truly see the favor of God working.

The waiting game isn't always easy, but it is always worth it. Why? Because we know that it will surely come to pass.

Morning Moment

Think about an area of your life where you have been waiting. Has it felt like delay or like development? Write down what God may be building in you during this season that you couldn't see before.

____

____

Prayer

Lord, teach me how to wait. Give me peace in the process and faith that what You promised will come to pass. I trust Your timing over my own. In Jesus' Name, Amen.

SECTION SIX

DAILY LIVING WITH GOD

Thirty

Fear NOT

For God has not given us a spirit of fear and timidity, but of power, love, and self-discipline. — 2 Timothy 1:7 NLT

Fear has a way of creating thoughts that destroy how we see ourselves and even how we view others. But God didn't give us that spirit. He gave us love, power, and—my favorite part—a *sound mind.*

Isn't it something that the verse ends with that phrase? Because a sound mind means stability, clarity, and peace. How can fear coexist with that? It can't. If your mind is full of soundness, there's no room for fear to take up residence. When we allow fear to live rent free, it often costs us in our thoughts, our perspectives, and ability to believe.

We've got to let go of what we pick up—the worry, the doubt, the fear—and hold tightly to what God *gave* us.

Lin-Manuel Miranda once said he realized he could either "fall underneath fear or stand on top of it." He described nerves as a *fuel source*—they'll either propel your ship or explode it. It's all about whether you stand on top of them or let them consume you.

That resonated with me. The next level always comes with discomfort—not because you're off track, but because God is stretching you beyond what's familiar. That's where faith steps in. I remember being stretched in some of the leadership roles while serving in the Navy. The truth is it was very uncomfortable. The truth is, that discomfort grew me far more than the comfortable places. I became more confident in my own abilities, increased my discernment and grew far beyond what I could have ever imagined.

Think about a time when you were being stretched, reflect on the fear you felt in that uncomfortable place, but also think about what it looked like on the other side of that.

So today, make the shift from fear to faith. Don't fall underneath it—stand on top of it. Use it as fuel to propel you toward what God has already destined for your life. The fear you feel isn't meant to paralyze you; it's meant to push you closer to purpose.

Morning Moment

Take a moment and think about where fear has gripped you. Write those things and reflect on what could come from no. longer fearing but thinking with a sound mind.

____

____

Prayer

Father, thank You for giving me power, love, and a sound mind. When fear rises, remind me that it's not from You. Help me to stand on top of it, using it as fuel to move forward in faith. Teach me to embrace discomfort as a sign of growth and trust You in every new season of "next." In Jesus' Name, Amen.

Thirty-One

Unpacking Life's Suitcase

Give your burdens to the Lord, and he will take care of you. He will not permit the godly to slip and fall. — Psalm 55:22 NLT

Give all your worries and cares to God, for he cares about you. — 1 Peter 5:7 NLT

Here we go again... another trip, another round of unpacking—just to pack again! You'd think I had some kind of problem with putting things back where they belong.

There I was, standing over not one, but *two* full suitcases from two trips ago—just staring. *SMH at myself.* That's when it hit me: maybe this isn't just about luggage. Maybe this says something about my walk with God.

See, I realized I'm quick to tuck things away until I absolutely must deal with them. I'll leave the bag zipped tight, out of sight, until the next trip comes around. Sound familiar?

But the truth is, many of us carry **emotional suitcases** we never unpack—disappointments, fears, guilt, unresolved pain. We keep them packed "just in case," never realizing how heavy they've become.

God, however, invites us to travel light. He tells us to *cast our cares on Him* because He cares for us. With God, there's no such thing as leaving your baggage packed for later. To walk with Him freely, you must **unpack daily** laying down every burden, every anxious thought, and every hidden hurt.

You can't go higher while still holding on to what He told you to release.

So today, grab those bags—spiritual, emotional, mental—and start unpacking. Empty them out and make yourself light for the next journey. Because with God, **you can't go if you don't unpack.**

Morning Moment

Consider what you need for your next get away. What do you need to take out of your bag? What do you need to add to your bag?

____

____

____

____

____

____

____

____

____

____

____

____

____

____

____

____

____

____

____

____

Prayer

Father, thank You for reminding me that You never called me to carry the weight of yesterday into today. Help me to unpack every care, burden, and hidden pain I've been holding onto. Teach me to release what no longer serves me and to trust You with the details of my journey. Lighten my load so I can walk freely into what You've prepared for me. In Jesus' Name, Amen.

Thirty-Two

Obedience Wins Every Time

Jesus replied, All who love me will do what I say. My Father will love them, and we will come and make our hone with each of them. —John 14:23 NLT

There are moments when obedience seems overly expensive. It requires levels of restraint that our natural man simply doesn't' want any part of. It requires patience and surrender that let's be honest, isn't always our first response, Yet Jesus makes it very clear that obedience isn't about you or me, but instead it is about our relationship or lack thereof with him.

Obedience is love in action!

When we make a choice to obey God, we are making a declaration of the desire to be with him. Obedience creates a dwelling place, a place of inhabitation with the father and his son. We think that to obey means to just do the right thing. No, it is greater than that, it is about making space for God to be nearby. It is making a habitation for him to trust that he can dwell perpetually.

Our Yes, will always bridge the gap to intimacy. Our Yes, will always open the doors that we can't seem to open ourselves. It is our Yes, that aligns us daily with the purpose of heaven. Even we don't understand it, obedience will always posture us for divine fellowship.

You may not always see it immediately and you may not always feel that it was the best choice, but obedience always wins!

God doesn't instruct us to do the easy things, but he gives us the ability to do just what needs to be done for not just us, but for others.

Don't overthink it, just do it! Put your trust in him and know that you win!

Morning Moment

Spend some time in prayer seeking God for what he wants you to be more obedient in. Allow him to speak to you and write down what is keeping you from obeying.

____

____

____

____

____

____

____

____

Prayer

Father, I know that if I obey, I will always win. Even when it looks like there is no victory, you have always rewarded obedience, Lord, in the areas that I am struggling to obey, teach me how to draw nearer to you. Teach me how to obey the first time because partial obedience is disobedience. In Jesus Name, Amen.

Thirty-Three

The Light at the End

Jesus spoke to the people once more and said, "I am the light of the world. If you follow me, you won't have to walk in darkness, because you will have the light that leads to life." —John 8:12 NLT

Have you ever been in a season where everything feels dim? You are making moves in the right direction, but clarity feels out of reach? You know you are headed somewhere, but you aren't sure where the path is leading you. It is in moments like this, we begin looking for the light at the end of the tunnel. Its hoping something head will finally make sense of this season that we have been in.

The good news is that Jesus promises that there is light; with him!

He tells us that, "if you follow me, you won't have to walk in darkness." That light isn't only at the end of the tunnel, but that the light Is on the path with us. Much like a flashlight, the light isn't always revealing everything along the way, but it will show us where to step next and sometimes, that is all we need to strengthen our faith along the way.

When we are in darkness, we are full of uncertainty, despair, frustration. But in the light, we find clarity, truth, and the way! When we follow Jesus, that doesn't negate us from stumbles or even falling, but we are guaranteed a way out. His light leads us out of darkness.

Think about the darkest room you've ever been in and then think about the way you felt when you got a glimpse of light. You felt relief, peace, joy, and safe. That is what it means to walk with the light daily. You may not know the way out, but you know that you are safe.

We often want to make it to the end of the tunnel so that we can come out, but it is in the daily walk with Jesus, we find how important it is to allow the light to lead us.

Morning Moment

Is there something keeping you from recognizing the light? What is it that is keeping you in darkness? Identify those things and ask God to show you how to daily expose them.

____

____

____

____

____

Prayer

Jesus, be the light in my life today. Where you lead me, I will follow. When I am unsure, I choose to follow you, When I am afraid because it seems dark, I will follow your light. In Jesus Name, A men.

Thirty-Four

Steer by the Seaman's Eye

Where there is no wise, intelligent guidance, the people fall and go off course like a ship without a helm. But in the abundance of [wise and godly] counselors there is victory. — Proverbs 11:14 AMP

"Steer by the seaman's eye" is a term used in ship navigation—it refers to steering a ship by sight, relying on wisdom and experience rather than instruments or electronics. The person at the helm must know how to read the water, sense direction, and stay steady through changing conditions. It's a skill learned only through time, trust, and experience. A skillset that a Sailor develops through time.

Proverbs reminds us that without wise and intelligent guidance, people lose direction—just like a ship without a helm. I spent many days out to sea, driving million-dollar Navy vessels, but it was only because of the guidance and wisdom of everyone apart of the team, we were able to stay on course and successfully navigate the seas.

Many are trying to steer this vessel called *life* without the counsel and wisdom that come from God. But steering by the seaman's eye requires more than natural vision—it demands *spiritual sight.* It means looking beyond what's immediately in front of you and trusting the One who charted the course.

God is the Captain. He knows every current, every wind, every unseen obstacle beneath the surface. Your role at the helm is to stay sensitive to His direction—to trust His chart and steer by faith, not by feeling.

The safest navigation doesn't come from our own understanding, but from the guidance of the Master Navigator who sees the end from the beginning.

So today, steer steady. Keep your eyes fixed on His wisdom, and you'll reach every destination safely—right on course.

Morning Moment

Who are you listening to while navigating through life? Has their voice been in alignment with the voice of God? The scriptures? Spend some time in prayer about those who help you navigate and ask God to give you others to align you in this next season.

____

____

____

____

Prayer

Father, thank You for being the captain of my life. Teach me how to steer with spiritual sight and to trust the wisdom You provide through Your Word and godly counsel. Keep me from drifting off course and help me stay aligned with the chart You've already prepared for me. In Jesus Name, Amen.

Thirty-Five

Morning Mercies

The faithful love of the Lord never ends! His mercies never cease. Great is his faithfulness; his mercies begin afresh each morning. — Lamentations 3:22–23 NLT

If you have made it to this final morning moment, I want you to know something—that in itself is a mercy.

There were mornings that brought you here heavy. Mornings where getting out of bed felt like an act of faith all on its own. Mornings where the weight of what you were carrying made it hard to believe that anything good was waiting on the other side of the day. And yet—here you are.

That is not by accident. That is mercy.

I have learned that the morning is holy ground. Long before the world wakes up and makes its demands, before the noise begins and the calendar fills and the weight of everything sets back in—there is a window. A sacred, quiet window where God meets you. Not because you have earned it. Not because you have it all together. But because His mercies are new. Every single morning. Without exception. Without condition. Without fail.

This is what Jeremiah discovered in one of the darkest books of the Bible. In the middle of lament—in the middle of grief and loss and the ruins of everything he had known—he stopped. And he remembered. *The faithful love of the Lord never ends.* Not never ended. Never ends. Present tense. Active. Right now. For you.

I began writing these morning moments on the deck of a Navy ship, watching the sun rise over open water with nothing between me and the horizon but the faithfulness of God. I did not always have the words. I did not always have the answers. But morning after morning, He met me there. In the ordinary. In the quiet. In the in-between.

And that is my prayer for you as you close this book.

That you would never again rush past a morning without remembering that it is a gift. That you would look for Him in the small things — the light breaking through your window, the breath in your lungs, the simple grace of a brand new day. That you would carry what you have learned in these thirty days not just into your mornings, but into every moment, every season, every ordinary miracle of your life.

He was faithful to bring you through every day that led to this one.

He will be faithful in every day that follows.

Great is His faithfulness. And it begins again—right now, this morning, for you.

Morning Moment

This final morning moment is yours completely. Use this space to write your own lamentation and prayer. Be honest with God about the mornings that were hard, the seasons that tested you, and the mercies that carried you through. Then close it with gratitude—for every sunrise, every promise kept, and every morning He met you right where you were.

____

____

Prayer

Lord, I come to this final morning with a full heart. I think of the mornings I almost didn't make it through—the ones heavy with grief, uncertainty, and doubt. And yet, You were there. Every single time, Your mercy was already waiting for me before I even opened my eyes.

Thank You for the mornings that broke me open and the ones that put me back together. Thank You for meeting me in the ordinary—in the quiet, in the commute, in the moments I almost missed You. Thank You for being a God who does not grow tired of showing up.

As I close this chapter, I ask that everything deposited in these thirty days would take root and grow. Let me carry Your presence into every room I enter, every relationship I hold, and every moment You have ordained for my life. Let me never stop looking for You in the everyday.

You are faithful. You have always been faithful. And great—so great—is that faithfulness. In Jesus' Name, Amen.

Acknowledgements

To my family, friends, and mentors—God has used each of you as instruments of grace in my life. Your investment in me, your prayers, your presence, and your encouragement have all been part of His greater plan. Because you poured, I found my vessels. Because you gave, I have something worth giving. Thank you, from the depths of my heart.

About the Author

Erica Triplett is a servant leader whose life has been shaped by two defining callings: service and encouragement. After twenty years in the United States Navy, she built a reputation not only for her leadership and discipline, but for her deep commitment to the people under her care—investing in their growth, walking alongside them through challenges, and championing their potential.

Now rooted in Chesapeake, Virginia, Erica continues that work as a minister at Faith World Ministries Inc., where she lives out its mission to change the world—through the Holy Spirit, one family at a time. She is the proud mother of two young adults pursuing higher education in the DMV region.

This book was born in the quiet—in the early morning hours she has long devoted to prayer, reflection, and renewal. It is out of those still, sacred moments with God that Erica found the words she hopes will meet you exactly where you are, and call you toward the fullest version of who you were created to be.

www.ingramcontent.com/pod-product-compliance
Lightning Source LLC
LaVergne TN
LVHW010913110826
845149LV00013B/2347

* 9 7 9 8 9 9 0 1 7 5 8 9 1 *